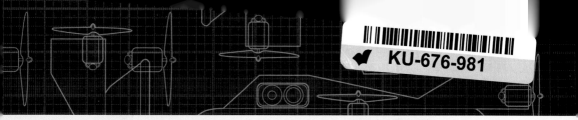

Plenum Chamber

The air pumped into the plenum chamber forms a ring that circulates around the base of the skirt, which helps to keep the air underneath from escaping.

More and more air is forced into the chamber all the time so the air underneath the hovercraft is at a higher pressure than the air outside. It's the air at a high pressure that raises the hovercraft and enables it to hover.

To maintain the lift, the engine and propeller or fan have to be sufficiently powerful to provide a high airflow rate into the chamber. The flow has to be greater than the amount of air that escapes from around the edges of the plenum chamber. The rate of air loss is not constant and there is no way of ensuring that any air escapes evenly all around the craft.

The plenum chamber enables the hovercraft to hover.

UNDERSTANDING AIR PRESSURE

If you want to get a clearer understanding of how air pressure works, try to squeeze a blown-up balloon. What happens? The balloon pushes back. This is because the air pressure in the balloon is higher than the air pressure outside.

Balance

When you let air out of the balloon and the internal and external pressures become equal, cancelling each other out, the balloon becomes limp. This principle is exactly the same for the human body. The pressure of Earth's atmosphere on us would crush our bodies if it wasn't counterbalanced by the equal internal pressure from the fluids inside us.

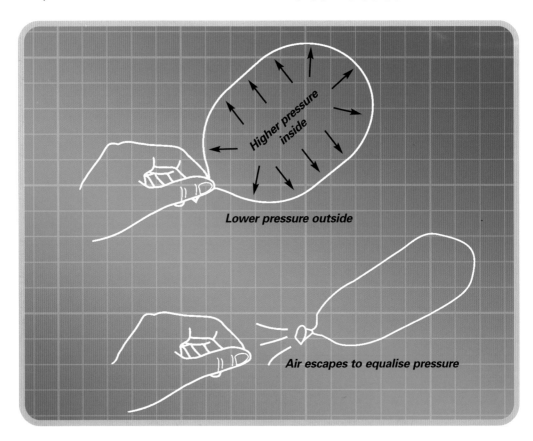

Higher pressure inside

Lower pressure outside

Air escapes to equalise pressure

LEARN ABOUT HOVER POWER

Written by David Holzer

TOPTHAT!Kids™

Copyright © 2005 Top That! Publishing plc,
Tide Mill Way, Woodbridge, Suffolk IP12 1AP, UK
www.topthatpublishing.com

WHAT IS A HOVERCRAFT?

A hovercraft, also known as an air cushion vehicle (ACV), is a vessel that rides on a cushion of air just above water, land or even ice. Today, the basic principle of the ACV is applied to everything from the largest to the smallest craft.

How Does a Hovercraft Work?

The way a hovercraft works is very simple. It usually has three basic components:

- a platform of some kind;
- a motorised fan with propellers; and
- a skirt.

Air is blown underneath the platform by one or more lift fans with propellers and trapped between the platform and the ground or water surface. This area of trapped air beneath the hovercraft is called a plenum chamber and can be up to 3 m thick.

propeller

air

fan

flexible skirt

Diver Down

Deep-sea divers experience huge additional pressure from the weight of the water above them when they're diving. The amount of air at high pressure inside their diving suit balances out the pressure from water. If this pressure isn't controlled when they rise to the surface, divers can experience an agonising condition called 'the bends'.

Deep-sea divers experience pressure in the same way as hovercraft.

Gravity

When the air pressure pushing the hovercraft upwards is precisely balanced with gravity pushing it downwards, it floats on a pillow of high-pressure air.

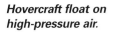

Hovercraft float on high-pressure air.

Only the edges of the hovercraft's skirt are actually touching the surface so it can't be steered like a car or an aeroplane. As there is so little friction between the hovercraft and the surface, it goes in the direction it's pushed.

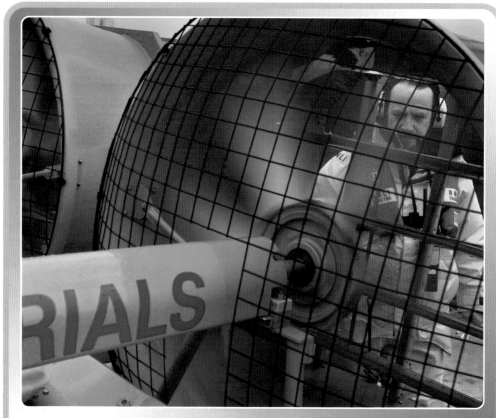

Hovercraft fan propellers push the craft forwards.

Most hovercraft are propelled by large fans attached to the rear that blow air backwards, so pushing the craft forwards. By putting a rudder behind the propellers to control the flow of air, the driver is able to steer using a handwheel. The turning movement of a hovercraft is called the 'yaw'.

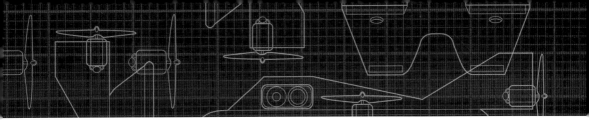

Fast and Slow

The speed the craft can move over water depends on wave height and wind speed. To speed up, the driver makes the fan turn more quickly which pushes more air backwards, behind the hovercraft. To slow down, the operator reverses the pitch of the propellers that move the vessel forwards, or changes the direction in which the air flows through the skirt vents.

To slow down, the operator may change the direction of airflow.

Typical single propulsion fan and aerodynamic rudders on a small hovercraft.

Water and Land

Whether on water or land, the vessel operates in pretty much the same way, with the air cushion preventing the hull from striking the surface when the terrain changes.

THE BEGINNINGS OF HOVERCRAFT

Although the first working hovercraft made its maiden voyage in 1956, there had been attempts to develop such a vessel almost 300 years before.

Swedenborg

The first attempts at designing a hovercraft were experiments to reduce the drag on boats and ships as they ploughed through water. Emanuel Swedenborg, a Swedish designer and philosopher, created the first recorded design for an air cushion vehicle in 1716.

Above: Replica of John Thornycroft's 1910 air-lubricated boat test tank model.

Right: The original John Thornycroft 1910 test tank model of an air-lubricated boat, which still has the original leather skirt.

Thornycroft

Then, in the mid 1870s, Sir John Thornycroft built various model craft, experimenting with 'air cushion' effects as he called them. He even filed patents involving air-lubricated hulls.

Energy

An operator would raise or lower a pair of oar-like air scoops. The downward strokes were meant to force compressed air underneath the hull, raising it above the surface. It was never built because it would take far more energy to operate than a single human could provide .

The hovercraft could not have existed without the invention of the internal combustion engine.

Invention

From then on, both Americans and Europeans began seriously trying to solve the problems of designing a hovercraft that actually worked. It wasn't until the late 19th century, with the invention of the internal combustion engine, that such a thing seemed possible.

For the first time, inventors had a means of achieving the high power-to-weight ratio necessary for hover flight.

· Torpedo

– Thornycroft built the first torpedo boat for the Royal Navy.

The hovercraft was invented by the British inventor Christopher Sydney Cockerell in 1956.

Inventor Sir Christopher Cockerell.

Britain. He discovered that two things dramatically reduced the performance of his boats:

- **Skin resistance**
  – the friction exerted by water moving over the surface of a boat.

- **Wave resistance**
  – energy being lost by a vessel having to batter its way through waves.

Cockerell was born in 1910. He worked for the Radio Research Company until 1935 and then for the Marconi Wireless Telegraph Company between 1936 and 1951. Cockerell was one of the team of remarkable scientists that helped develop radar, which Winston Churchill believed played a vital part in the outcome of WWII.

Resistance

In the early 1950s, Cockerell was running a small boat yard on the Norfolk Broads in

Christopher Cockerell testing the model in a dyke at Somerleyton, Suffolk.

Bertin's experiments evolved into this French hovercraft.

Air Lubrication

Cockerell began to develop the old idea of 'air lubrication' – remember Sir John Thornycroft? – which had yet to be made to work. Jean Bertin, a French engineer, was exploring similar ideas around the same time. The aim was to reduce friction between water and the vehicle – called hydraulic drag – using air lubrication.

He began with a punt, then used a 20-knot ex-naval launch as a test craft.

French engineer Jean Bertin.

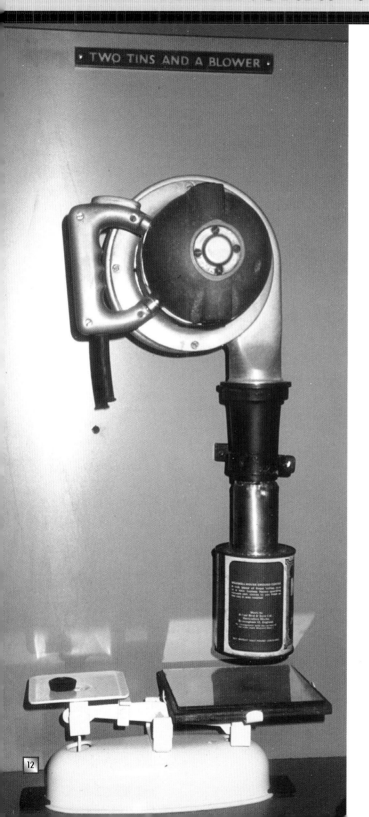

· TWO TINS AND A BLOWER ·

Testing

To test his ideas, Cockerell put a cat food tin inside a coffee tin and used an industrial air blower to blow air into them. Using a set of kitchen scales, he found out that the thrust produced when one can was inside the other was greater than when air was blown into one can only.

Knighted

For his achievement, recognised as one of the most brilliant inventions of the 20th century, Christopher Cockerell was knighted in 1969. Throughout the 1970s, he was involved in the development of wave power.

A replica of Sir Christopher Cockerell's initial tin experiment.

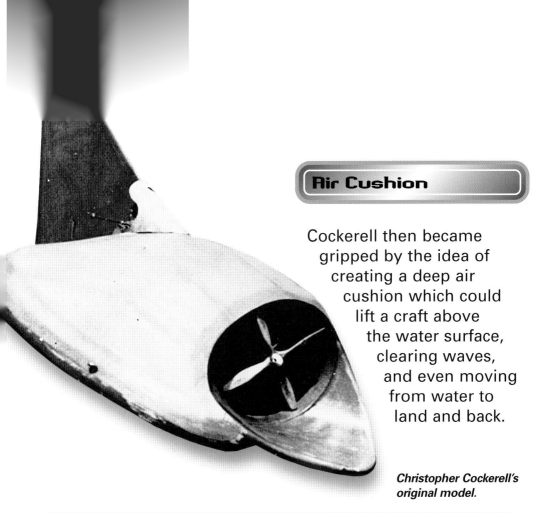

Air Cushion

Cockerell then became gripped by the idea of creating a deep air cushion which could lift a craft above the water surface, clearing waves, and even moving from water to land and back.

Christopher Cockerell's original model.

The original model operating 'round the pole' over grass.

Saunders-Roe

In 1956, this experiment led to the first hovercraft to be produced commercially. It was called the SR.N1 (Saunders Roe Nautical One) after the company that developed it. An improved version, with the addition of a flexible skirt to retain the air cushion, was developed in 1958.

Hovercraft Car Ferry

The first SR.N1 successfully crossed the English Channel – from Dover to Calais – in July 1959. This was around the 50th anniversary of the first Channel crossing in an aeroplane by Louis Blériot. It made the crossing in a remarkable 35 minutes, far faster than a traditional boat.

The Saunders-Roe hovercraft.

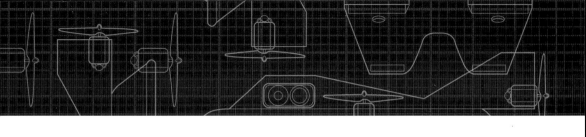

The twin-propeller SR.N6 Mk 6 hovercraft.

Passengers

The principles discovered in experiments with the SR.N1 meant that better craft could be developed. The technological advances allowed a craft, the SR.N6, to be built which could move passengers securely at a maximum speed of 56 knots.

Two SR.N6 hovercraft called *Swift* and *Sure*, were brought into passenger service for the 45 km Ramsgate to Calais route. Some technical problems and bad weather conditions meant that the service lasted less than three months. However, these early attempts led to some more successful hovercraft.

Hovercraft are unique because they are amphibious, which means that they can go where traditional cars and boats can't – from land to water and back.

All Terrain

Air cushion designs have proved useful in climates that would otherwise be difficult, or impossible, to navigate. Swamps, marshes, lakes, rivers, snow-covered fields, coral reefs, frozen lakes and muddy bogs have been overcome by hovercraft-type vehicles able to carry or pull heavy loads.

Land

Hovercraft can travel over most terrain in almost all conditions, including grass up to 2 m tall. They can travel over farmland and fields because, although they press down the product, they will not harm the ground itself. This means that hovercraft can run on many surfaces that are

A female Navy sailor directing Landing Craft Air Cushion troop transport off the shore and back to the USS Bataan.

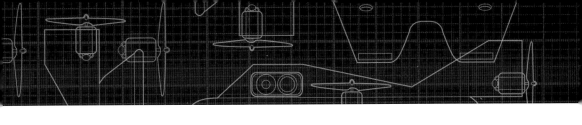

The British AP1-88 hovercraft on ice.

inaccessible to other vehicles. Hovercraft are environmentally friendly because they don't leave a wake that disturbs fragile sea beds or trails on land.

Water Power

Hovercraft can travel over water with no concern for depth or hidden obstacles. They will go against the current of a river with no speed reduction. Hovercraft are especially useful for search and rescue operations when other forms of transport are inadequate – during floods when boats cannot risk the strong currents and torrential rain, for example.

Hazardous Conditions

Hovercraft operate effectively in hazardous conditions, such as over thin and broken ice. While there are conditions where it is difficult, if not impossible, for conventional boats to navigate, hovercraft can operate from unprepared river banks and beaches as well as from piers, pontoons and harbours, and in climates from the Arctic to the tropics.

A propeller is a mechanical device, essentially a screw, that produces force or thrust along an axis of rotation when it is rotated in either air or water.

Propeller Blades

A propeller pulls itself through the air in the same way that a bolt pulls itself through a nut. Simple propellers are made of two, three or four blades and each of these is a section of a helix.

A simple hovercraft with one large propeller.

Propellers designed to work in air differ from those for use in water. Helicopter blades, for example, are thin and shaped like an aerofoil if you look at them in a cross-section, while boat blades are extremely broad but thin.

Nearly all ships, as well as hovercraft, use a propeller, as do most aircraft.

Propulsion Units

The propulsion units on a hovercraft consist of an engine for each propeller. The engine must provide enough power to turn the propeller at a high enough speed for it to draw in air. This air is then forced out of the back of the propeller to provide the thrust to move the hovercraft along.

Above: The number of propellers on hovercraft varies.

This ice-breaking hovercraft can rotate its four propellers independently for better control.

Multiple Propellers

The number of propellers fitted to a hovercraft can also vary. Small recreational and racing hovercraft generally have a single propeller. However, large military hovercraft and those used to transport passengers and other vehicles generally have multiple propellers. For example, on the SR.N4 cross-channel hovercraft there are four four-bladed propellers at 5.8 m in diameter!

Ducted propulsion fan on a Bill Baker vehicles BBV-6.

Blade Sizes

The size of propellers used on hovercraft can vary enormously. Some small one-person hovercraft have propellers consisting of blades of about 2.75 m in diameter, whilst the blades of large car and passenger ferry hovercraft propellers can be up to 6 m in length.

A blade from a 6 m propeller as used on the SR.N4 Mk III and BH.7 hovercraft, on display at the Hovercraft Museum, Hampshire.

Steering

On the SR.N4, the pylons on which the propellers are mounted can be rotated to change the direction of thrust and, therefore, the direction of the hovercraft. On smaller craft that use a single propeller, rudders control direction.

MODERN HOVERCRAFT

Hovercraft today come in a wide variety of shapes and sizes, from individual hoverboards to huge hoverbarges.

Air Cushion Vehicles

Some air cushion vehicles, such as the Bertin Hovertruck, travel over roads and solid ground using ordinary wheel systems. When they move over marshland, a built-in air cushion system supports some of the vehicle's weight. The aerotrain, an experimental air cushion vehicle designed to run on a track similar to a monorail, reached a speed of 346 km/h on a test track in France. It rode on a cushion of air 0.25 cm thick.

Lightweight Hovercraft

Many countries have extensive coastlines and offshore islands where there is shallow water around the

The aerotrain was the first train to travel on a cushion of air.

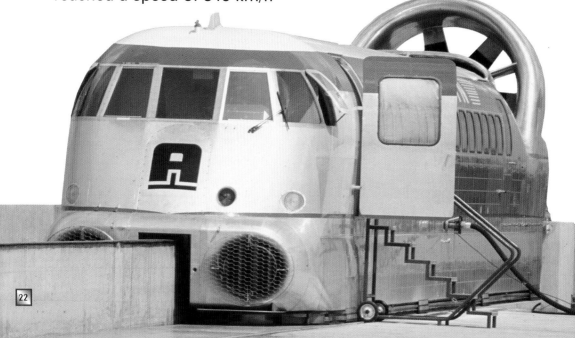

22

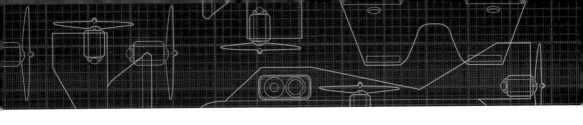

The **Princess Margaret** *car and passenger ferry.*

shoreline. These are ideal locations for hovercraft, which can be equipped for search and rescue operations as well as intercepting vessels engaged in criminal activity.

Interception

Hovercraft are able to lie up, maybe hidden under trees on a beach. They can then move out to intercept criminals very rapidly, over land, extremely shallow water, sand, rocks and mud – intercepting in the quickest straight line.

They can also operate as conventional craft, using berths, piers and pontoons.

Large Hovercraft

The world's largest air cushion vehicles were the two 330-tonne SR.N4 Mark 3 hovercraft. These, the *Princess Margaret* and the *Princess Anne*, operated in the English Channel from 1968 to 2000. They travelled at a speed of 65 knots (120 km/h) and carried up to 400 passengers and 50 cars.

COMBAT HOVERCRAFT

Lightweight, highly mobile hovercraft are used by forces such as the British Royal Marines, US Marines and Russian Marines in military situations when rapid movement to, and across, beaches is vital.

In this way, troops on ships can be carried straight onto landing beaches without having to unload in vulnerable areas.

US Army Combat Hovercraft SK-5 Gun Boat

Vietnam War

As Vietnam is surrounded by long coastlines and contains vast river systems, US forces wanted to use anything that floated to reach the country.

Everything from surfboards to the immensely powerful carrier forces were used, but hovercraft played an important role.

The SK-5 hovercraft was extensively used in Vietnam for patrol and missions in the Mekong Delta. It could travel with equal ease over both water and land. The M-5 RACV (Reconnaissance Air Cushion Vehicle) is a modern development of the SK-5.

An American SK-5 operating in Vietnam.

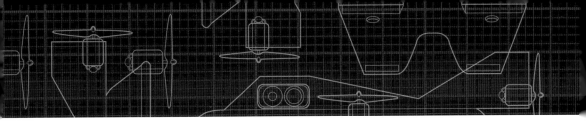

Protection

Hovercraft are capable of operating in areas that are difficult, or impossible, for other military equipment to access. This makes them useful for border protection, anti-arms, drugs and weapons smuggling and anti-terrorism and anti-piracy duties.

Hovercraft are capable of operating in areas that are difficult for other military equipment to access.

Lightweight hovercraft are used by Marines.

COMBAT HOVERCRAFT

British Royal Navy BH.7

The BH.7 is the only large British military hovercraft left in existence and the only one built for the UK. The BH.7 demonstrated significant military advances in the use of hovercraft. Designed as a reliable, high-performance military vehicle, it could go anywhere as it was not dependent on ports, harbours or deep water. It could be deployed and camouflaged on any suitable beach and

• Military Craft
– Military hovercraft can achieve higher speeds with greater payloads than any craft in their class

with a reaction time of two minutes, it was superior to anything of its day. It could operate over any terrain and deliver troops onto many beaches which otherwise could not have been reached.

The BH.7 was built exclusively for the UK.

Landing Craft Air Cushions can carry loads of up to 70 tonnes.

LCAC

The US Navy Landing Craft Air Cushion (LCAC) is a high-speed, over-the-beach, fully amphibious landing craft capable of carrying a 55–70 tonne payload. It is used to transport weapons systems, equipment, cargo and personnel from ship to shore and across the beach. The advantages of air-cushion landing craft are numerous.

Equipment

They can carry heavy loads, such as an M-1 tank, at high speeds. Their load capacity and speed mean more people can reach the shore in a shorter time over fewer trips. The air cushion allows this vehicle to reach more than seventy per cent of the world's coastline, while conventional landing craft can land at only fifteen per cent.

PASSENGER HOVERCRAFT

Experimental

The world's first experimental passenger hovercraft service took place in the summer of 1962. The 24-seat Vickers VA 3 hovercraft ran for two months and crossed the Dee Estuary in North Wales. However, bad weather conditions meant that almost half of its operational days were cancelled.

The Vickers VA 3 hovercraft operated the world's first passenger service in 1962.

First Service

An actual passenger service was started in the same year. In August, 1962, passengers could travel by hovercraft from Portsmouth to Ryde on the Isle of Wight. The SR.N2 craft used for the service had 48 seats and was much larger and more robust than the Vickers VA 3.

*The **Princess Anne** – the first hovercraft to be extended to a full SR.N4 Mk III size.*

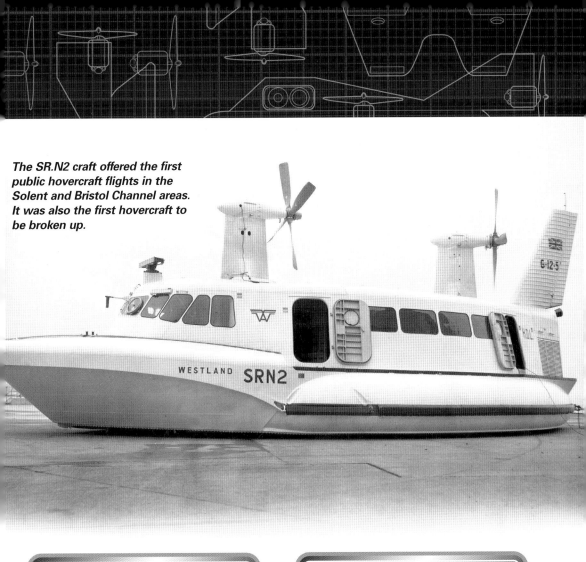

The SR.N2 craft offered the first public hovercraft flights in the Solent and Bristol Channel areas. It was also the first hovercraft to be broken up.

WESTLAND SRN2

Channel Crossing

A prototype SR.N4 named *Princess Margaret* entered commercial service on the cross-Channel route from Dover, England to Boulogne, France on 1st August, 1968. The following year a second SR.N4 called the *Princess Anne* joined the cross-Channel fleet. This craft went on to set a new cross-Channel record in 1995 when it reached Dover from Calais in just 22 minutes.

End of an Era

Sadly, the two SR.N4 hovercraft were finally retired from service on 1st October, 2000. The high maintenance and fuel costs meant that the hovercraft could not compete with ferries and the Channel Tunnel. These two hovercraft transported over 80 million passengers and more than 11 million cars across the Channel during their thirty-year service.

If you thought that hoverboards only existed in science fiction, think again! The first commercial single-person hoverboard scooter, called the Airboard, has been invented by Kevin Inkster.

Science Fiction?

A hoverboard scooter, otherwise known as the Airboard.

The Airboard uses the same air cushion principles to glide above the ground as conventional hovercraft but

Airboards are made up of:

- an engine and fan suspended under the shell to provide the air cushion and thrust;

- a fibreglass platform for the rider to stand on;

- a rubber skirt used to form an air cushion under the vehicle;

- a friction drive wheel that comes into contact with the ground and provides added acceleration; and

- a handlebar with two control levers, one for the engine/fan speed and the other for the friction drive clutch.

is ridden standing up. It uses a drive wheel, which touches the ground, to accelerate.

Surfaces

Airboards are meant to be ridden on level ground but have been proven to glide over other surfaces including grass, concrete and asphalt. They don't have the power to ride over bodies of water.

To stop an Airboard, simply turn off the engine for it to slowly come to a halt, just like a traditional hovercraft.

The Airboard glides over surfaces including grass, concrete and asphalt.

Airboard – a one-person hovercraft!

Air cushion

The cushion of air underneath the shell of the Airboard is provided by the fan, which also provides a stream of air which exits through the back of the vehicle to create thrust.

The Airboard is controlled as a skateboard or surfboard, by shifting weight from side to side. The drive wheel is activated when weight is shifted backwards. It's also possible to execute 360-degree turns.

Although you may not think it, there are some famous hovercraft in films.

Die Another Day

In this twentieth Bond film, one of the most exciting scenes sees a spectacular hovercraft chase through minefields which ends with Bond's capture and imprisonment by enemy forces.

A character ends up pinned to a speeding hovercraft before plunging over a raging waterfall.

Back to the Future

In a futuristic tie to the original *Back to the Future,* the sequel (*Back to the Future II*) featured airborne hoverboards.

• Star Wars

– Although a fantasy film, the *Star Wars* collection contains technology which was advanced for its time.

– Luke Skywalker's landspeeder, for example, compares to current hovercraft.

Many people thought these were real, but they were just boards glued to the actors' feet, enhanced by lots of special effects.

James Bond tests the speed limit of a hovercraft in Die Another Day.

The Matrix

There are several hovercraft in the *Matrix* trilogy of films and short films associated with them. In *The Matrix*, Morpheus' hovercraft is called Nebuchadnezzar. Under attack from the Machine Army in *The Final Flight of the Osiris*, the rebel warriors aboard the hovercraft *Osiris* attempt to send a vital message to the citizens of Zion, the last human city on Earth.

HOW TO BUILD YOUR OWN HOVERCRAFT

This experiment can be done without the sticky putty and cotton reel if you push the neck of the balloon through the hole in the middle of an old CD, but it won't work as well.

The Balloon Hovercraft

1. Stretch the neck of the balloon over one end of the cotton reel – you should be able to blow up the balloon through the hole in the middle of the cotton reel. Don't do this bit yet!

You will need:
- an uninflated balloon
- an old compact disc
- a cotton reel
- sticky putty

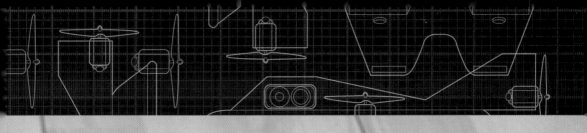

2. Stick a ring of sticky putty to the free side of the cotton reel. Do not let the sticky putty block the hole in the centre of the reel. Line up the hole in the cotton reel with the hole in the middle of the CD. Firmly press the cotton reel and the CD together.

3. Blow up the balloon through the hole in the CD. You might find this a bit difficult as the CD will be right in your face!

4. Now place the CD on a smooth, flat surface and give it a gentle push. It should float like a hovercraft! Of course, real hovercraft aren't powered by balloons inflated above them.

DECORATING YOUR OWN HOVERCRAFT

You may find it surprising to learn that people race hovercraft. Of course, these aren't the huge vehicles used to carry people and cars but small craft that take one or two people.

Racing

Racing hovercraft are decorated like any sporting vehicle. This means that they have colourful, bright designs so that it's easy to tell them apart when they're racing at high speeds. They're also covered with the logos of companies who sponsor them. Being sponsored is often how a racing team has the money to buy and maintain their vehicle. It's also a way for drivers to be paid for racing. Maybe you can get your parents to sponsor you!

Racing hovercraft have colourful, bright designs.

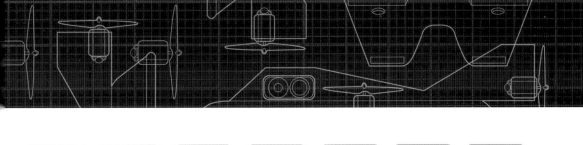

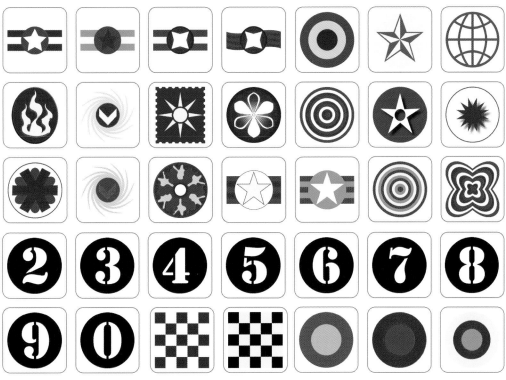

Decorate your craft with bright designs or logos such as these shown above. You can create your own unique hovercraft to race against those of your friends.

Colourful

You can turn your hovercraft into a racing machine by decorating it with bright designs and numbers. To make it look as though it has been sponsored, look for logos on products in adverts in old comics and magazines, cut them out and stick them on the balloon, or copy them on using permanent markers. The most important thing is to make

• Marker pens

– Use permanent marker pens on your balloons otherwise the ink may rub off!

your hovercraft look as different as possible from anyone else's.

Now you're ready to race your hovercraft!

RACING YOUR MODEL HOVERCRAFT

As you'll be racing over a fixed distance with no tricky turns or obstacles, the only way to win a race is by going faster than everyone else. How can you make your balloon model hovercraft go faster?

Bigger Balloon

Of course, you could use a bigger balloon than anyone else, but you need to be careful as this might be so big that your hovercraft won't stay on the ground, or it might tip over.

More Balloons

You can experiment with building a bigger hovercraft that uses two or more balloons. Remember, however, that so can the people you're racing against. Also, the more balloons you use the bigger

A hovercraft can easily make the transition from water to land.

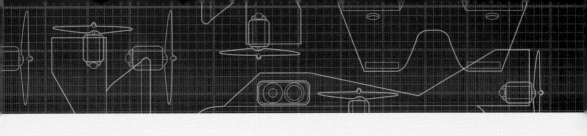

your hovercraft has to become and it then gets harder to control.

Hole Size

The best way to increase the speed of your hovercraft is by experimenting with the size of the hole through which the air from the balloon escapes. The wider this is, the faster the air escapes and the quicker the hovercraft will go. Your problem is to be able to tell how quickly, or slowly, the air needs to escape for your hovercraft to go the whole distance of the racecourse.

Experiment

The last thing you want to happen is for it to go faster than everyone else's at first and then to run out of steam halfway down the course. The only way to do it is by experimenting until the air escapes at the right speed for it to go fast enough to complete the course and win. When you conduct this kind of experiment you're dealing with the same kind of challenge faced by the first inventors of the hovercraft.

You will need to practise before you beat others, just like real racers.

REAL-LIFE RACING HOVERCRAFT

Many people become obsessed with hovercraft and it's easy to see why! People who like hovercraft often go on to race them.

Hovercraft Races

Hovercraft races are run on a track that mixes land and water, usually involving tight turns and fast straight sections. Hovercraft racing can feel very fast when you have nothing underneath you, especially as the craft is affected by wind very easily. When there is oncoming wind and you are travelling at speed, the craft tends to lift at the front. This is known as the wheelie effect.

Hovercraft racing in Lucon, France.

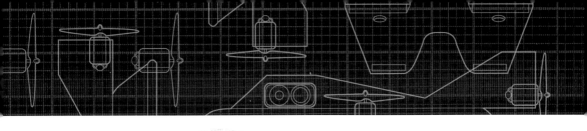

You can become involved in racing from the age of eleven.

WHF

The World Hovercraft Federation was formed in 1986. In their championship, racers from all over the world compete every two years. They race to find out who can go the fastest over land and water.

Young Starters

One of the most exciting things about hovercraft racing is that you can begin from the age of eleven, although for some of the classes you have to be sixteen.

Junior Manoeuvres

Before a new junior driver can take part in their first Formula Junior Race, they are required to pass a simple manoeuvrability test and answer a number of questions based on the operation of their craft. The manoeuvrability tests are designed to ensure that the young driver can operate the craft in a safe and effective manner in a racing environment. Questions are included to confirm the driver's understanding of the regulations.

REAL-LIFE RACING HOVERCRAFT

Modern Sporting Hovercraft

With this kind of hovercraft racing, the teams use lightweight hovercraft that can go as fast as 105 km/h. They have no brakes, which means that competitors must either turn round or wipeout (crash) to stop. The vehicles have 120-horsepower engines, which means that competitors also have to be careful that they don't take off!

Steering

The driver steers by using rudders in the airflow and by moving their body. As there is little or no friction with the surface the driver is moving over, the problem is making sure that the hovercraft doesn't move with the wind.

Rudders

All types of craft use rudders in the propulsion airflow for direction control. The driver operates the rudder by either

Racers have to make sure the hovercraft don't move with the wind.

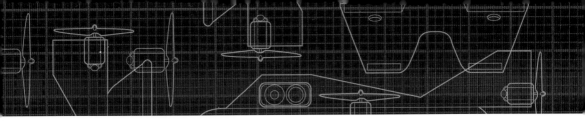

A single-seat racing hovercraft.

a deck-mounted joystick (not very popular now) or a cycle handlebar arrangement. The engines are usually controlled by lever-type throttles mounted on the handlebars.

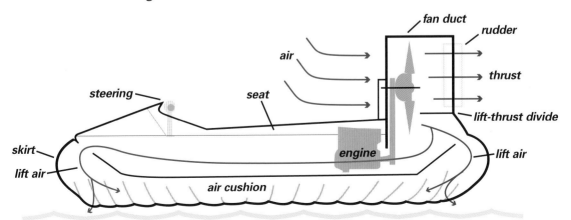

fan duct

rudder

air

thrust

lift-thrust divide

steering

seat

skirt

lift air

engine

lift air

air cushion

Cross-section of a single-engine integrated hovercraft.

REAL-LIFE RACING HOVERCRAFT

Engine

Where hovercraft once used two engines – one in the front for lift and the other for thrust – modern sporting hovercraft only use a single engine/fan setup to do both jobs. Hovercraft require engines which develop high power and are constructed from light, durable materials, which is why 2-stroke engines are mostly used.

Bigger and Faster

When hovercraft are raced, they are split into different categories based on engine

FORMULA 1
Total engine capacity over 500 cc

FORMULA 2
Engine capacity between 250 cc and 500 cc

FORMULA 3
Engine capacity under 250 cc

FORMULA JUNIOR
Engine capacity under 250 cc

FORMULA 25
Engine capacity maximum 25 hp

Hovercraft racing at Claydon House in Buckinghamshire.

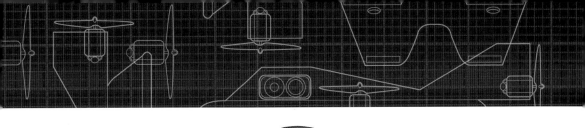

size. These are the engine sizes allowed in each class: in F1, people use racing snow mobile engines. F1s have separate lift and thrust engines, usually 250 cc lift and a very large thrust engine; in F2, most people use microlight engines and these hulls (bodies) are integrated as well; and in F3, most people use 2-stroke motorbike engines, and these hulls are also integrated.

When hovercrafts are raced, they are split into different categories based on engine size.

Body

The hovercraft hull can be constructed from plywood, fibreglass or even aluminium. It is important that it is as light as possible and incorporates buoyancy to enable it to float should it stop on water. Most are made from fibreglass. The weight can vary from 129 kg to a dual-engined F1 craft which can easily exceed 200 kg.

Skirt

The skirt's purpose is to retain the cushion of air which supports the hovercraft. Skirt material must be light and able to withstand adverse conditions such as stones and sand. Skirts cannot pop. At the bottom of each skirt there is a large hole through which the air escapes.

• Hover technology

– Flymo lawnmowers work on the same principles as hovercraft.

HOVERCRAFT OF THE FUTURE

Hovercraft are extremely environmentally friendly. Despite its size, a large commercial hovercraft can go over an egg without breaking it! This is why many people think that small, personal hovercraft may well replace cars and other vehicles one day.

Science Fiction

Although this might sound like science fiction, we've already discovered hoverboards and seen how they work.

Moller has tried to invent personal hovercraft for use in the future.

People are becoming increasingly convinced that hovercraft could travel high off the ground.

US inventor Paul Moller developed the Skycar, a mix of car and aeroplane.

This would mean that there would be no reason for expensive road systems that damage the environment and cause pollution. Hovercraft could dock at huge hover ports high up in the air.

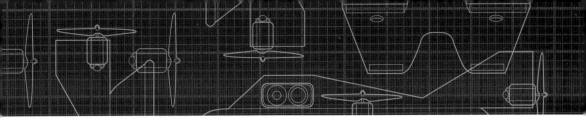

A future police patrol vehicle?

GPS

Individual hovercraft might be long and narrow so that they could navigate in the air easily. They could be controlled by Global Positioning Satellites (GPS). These are satellites in space that enable people to find out where they are and to navigate. They're commonly used at sea and in modern cars. There might even be one in your parents' car.

Smart Roads

With GPS it's even possible to have vehicles that don't have to be steered manually. The satellite does all the work. You just tell the satellite where you want to go. This technology has already been developed and tested on 'smart' roads and cars. Imagine flying your own hovercraft high in the air, being automatically flown to the beach!

CHALLENGING THE WORLD HOVERCRAFT SPEED RECORD

A competitor in the British Hovercraft Championships.

Speed

In March 1964, the world's first hovercraft race was held at Lake Burley Griffin in the Australian capital city of Canberra. Every year since then hovercraft enthusiasts have raced there to try to break the record.

Today, the record stands at 137.399 km/h. This was recorded on September 20th 1995 by the American Bob Windt in a V-6 auto engine-powered UH19P.